GW01463880

THE
GENTLEMAN USHER
OF THE BLACK ROD

Maurice Bond and David Beamish

LONDON

HER MAJESTY'S STATIONERY OFFICE

Acknowledgement: to the Central Office of Information
for the preparation and supply of illustrations.

Front cover. Lieutenant-General Sir David House, GCB, CBE, MC
Gentleman Usher of the Black Rod

ISBN 0 11 700567 3

The Gentleman Usher
of The Black Rod

The Gentleman Usher of the Black Rod—to give Black Rod his full title—is an officer of the Order of the Garter and also of the House of Lords. As an officer of the Order of the Garter he takes part in the Garter ceremonies held annually at Windsor; as an officer of the House of Lords he takes a leading part in Parliamentary ceremonial and also has the full-time job of supervising the administration of that section of the Palace of Westminster allocated to the House of Lords, and of controlling the admission of visitors to the House.

To many people Black Rod is known only as a slightly mysterious ceremonial officer who summons the House of Commons to hear the Queen's Speech at the Opening of Parliament. The aim of this booklet is to give a fuller idea of who Black Rod is and what he does, and to provide an account of the origins and history of his office.

The origins of the office of Black Rod

Black Rod is first mentioned in connection with his Parliamentary duties in the early sixteenth century, but his work as an officer of the Order of the Garter can be traced back considerably further, almost to the establishment of the Order.

In 1348 King Edward III, soon after his military triumphs at Crécy and Calais, founded an order of chivalry, the 'Most Noble Order of the Garter', comprising himself and 25 of the leading Knights of the day. Their patron saint was St. George, and at or around his feast day, 23rd April, the Knights assembled at Windsor for three days in order to participate in a sequence of services in the Chapel, discussions and elections of new Knights in their Chapter House (now the Deanery) and feasts in the royal apartments in the Upper Ward. Processions were an important part of the festivals. As the Knights moved from one point to another of the Castle they were led by an usher who carried a black rod, and when they arrived at their destination he 'kept the doors' (i.e. denied admission to those not entitled to be present)—this gave him the name of 'usher', for *ussarius* was mediaeval latin for door-keeper.

The earliest known reference to such an usher of the Order is in letters patent of the year 1361, which granted 12d a day for life to Walter Whitehorse, described as 'usher of the free chapel in Wyndesore Castle', as his salary for bearing the rod in processions on feast days. It seems almost certain that Walter Whitehorse was the first 'Black Rod' (though the usher was not originally so described) and that he had acted as usher for some time before 1361—a house had been built for him in Windsor Castle in 1353, and this house seems to have become a perquisite of the usher's office. Walter Whitehorse was one of the King's yeomen at the time of his appointment and, as will be seen, Black Rod has remained a member of the Royal Household to this day. At the moment, in addition to the Gentleman Usher of the Black Rod the Household includes a Gentleman Usher to the Sword of State, 9 other Gentlemen Ushers and 12 Extra Gentlemen Ushers.

It is known from the terms of their appointments that early holders of the office of Black Rod had the duty of carrying the rod at Garter processions, but the earliest detailed account of Black Rod's duties comes in the statutes relating to the Officers of the Order of the Garter which were enacted in about 1522. The statute relating to the Usher explains the purpose of the Black Rod—it was carried in lieu of a mace, as a symbol of authority, empowering the usher to arrest those offending against the Statutes and Ordinances of the Order of the Garter. Any knight who was to be degraded from the order was touched with the Rod, and for this the Usher received a fee of five pounds. Twenty shillings had to be paid by any Knight Companion admonished by the Usher for a lesser offence. Newly elected Knights had to pay ten shillings to the Usher. The Statute then provided that, for the dignity and honour of the order, the Usher was to be 'chief of all the Ushers of this Kingdom' and that, if not a knight, he should be knighted on appointment. This certainly had not always been customary, and later in the sixteenth century the practice lapsed; however, Black Rod has always been a knight or has received knighthood since the time of Charles II.

Black Rod has continued his service to the Knights of the Garter down to the present day, and now each year, in June, when Her Majesty The Queen and other members of the Order walk in procession from the royal apartments in the Upper Ward to St. George's Chapel in the Lower Ward at Windsor they are accompanied by Black Rod wearing his Garter mantle (*see plate 1*).

Black Rod and Parliament

Initially the duties of Black Rod within the Order of the Garter must have been comparatively light. The earliest known reference to further duties is in the Garter statute of 1522 (already referred to), which specified an additional responsibility, to keep the doors 'in the High Court called the Parliament'. One theory is that when King Henry VIII moved from the Palace of Westminster, where his residence had been, to the Palace of Whitehall, his chief usher remained at Westminster to act as usher to the House of Lords. Unfortunately the records of Tudor Parliaments are sparse and give no indication until the early seventeenth century of what in fact the work of Black Rod entailed. Certainly Black Rod did not confine himself in the sixteenth century to Parliamentary work: Sir William Compton (in the year he was

PLATE 1 : *Black Rod, Sir Brian Horrocks (right), takes part in the Garter ceremonies at St. George's Chapel, Windsor Castle.*

appointed Black Rod) was fighting in the French campaigns and subsequently attended Henry VIII at the Field of the Cloth of Gold. Compton served in the Scottish war of 1523, and died 'immensely rich, leaving property in eighteen counties'. His successor, Henry Norris, was Groom of the Stole to Queen Anne Boleyn and constable of two castles but, although he seems to have promoted Henry's marriage with Lady Jane Seymour, he was suspected of an intrigue with Anne Boleyn and was tried at Westminster Hall. He has the unhappy distinction of being the only Black Rod to die by execution. A more successful Black Rod, and perhaps the most notable of all Tudor holders of the office, was Sir Philip Hoby, Black Rod from 1543 to 1554, who while in office served as Ambassador in Flanders. Like his half-brother, Sir Thomas, who translated Castiglione's *Book of the Courtier,* he was a scholar, and was also a friend of Titian and of Aretino. Hoby's portrait was drawn by Holbein, and he is commemorated by a superb monument in Bisham church.

Black Rod in the seventeenth and eighteenth centuries

The official Journals of the House of Lords, which date from the beginning of the reign of Henry VIII, first mention Black Rod in 1601. Mr. Coningsby, described as 'the Gentleman Usher of the House', is recorded as complaining that in the previous Parliament the Serjeant-at-Arms (an officer attending the Lord Chancellor) had been sent to bring persons before the House for breach of privilege. This function, he claimed, 'did appertain to his Place'. A Committee looked into the matter but it was not until 1640 that the House decided that 'all Warrants for apprehending of Delinquents and bringing them before this Honourable Court' should be directed to Black Rod. This duty was for a time after 1660 again shared with the Serjeant-at-Arms. Since 1828 the House has almost invariably employed Black Rod to apprehend delinquents, though for a long time he has not been required to do so.

From its foundation to Coningsby's time, the office of Black Rod appears to have been given to someone who was already a member of the Royal Household. However, James I granted the office in reversion (that is, when it should next fall vacant) to James Maxwell, a grant which did not please the Gentlemen Ushers of the Court, who claimed that the office had always belonged to their body. In 1631 it was decreed that in future the office should always go to one of the Gentlemen Ushers, to be appointed by the King. However, at the outbreak of the Civil War Maxwell succeeded in 1642 in getting letters patent passed appointing him and Alexander Thayne as joint holders of the office. But, subsequently, the King appointed Peter Newton, the eldest Gentleman Usher, to be Black Rod. As a result, during the Civil War the division between Parliament and King was reflected in a division in the office of Black Rod—the Garter duties were carried out by Peter Newton, a member of the Royal Household, while in Parliament Maxwell and Thayne were recognised as holding the office of Black Rod. Certainly there was plenty for Black Rod to do in Parliament. In 1642 the House had to pay him 'extraordinary expenses' of £603. 12s—he had served 526 orders of the House on individuals in London alone and had journeyed as far around as the Welsh coast and Lancashire in order to effect arrests.

It is during the early seventeenth century that the earliest references to Black Rod's duty of summoning the Commons to attend the Sovereign in the House of Lords may be found. In 1614 the Commons Journal records that Coningsby came to let the Commons know that the King had called for them. On one occasion in 1628, when James Maxwell was Black Rod, a Mr. Crane

4

went to summon the Commons. The Commons Journal records that 'it was very ill taken, that Mr. Maxwell, Knight of the Black Rod, did not come himself to bring this message, as had formerly been used'. In 1641 it is recorded that 'Mr. Maxwell, coming to the House, with a Message, without his black Rod; and coming in, before he was called in; Exception was taken at both'. This is the first indication in the Commons Journals of what became the custom of not admitting Black Rod until he had knocked three times. Charles I's attempted arrest of the 'five members' in January 1642 may well have led the Commons to guard more jealously their right not to be interfered with by the Sovereign or his representative—which is today manifested by a ritual slamming of the door in Black Rod's face. (The ceremony is described in detail on pages 12 and 13 below.)

When Thayne first attended the House in 1642, it was as deputy to James Maxwell, to act in his absence. This is the first record of a deputy for Black Rod in his capacity as usher of the House of Lords. The Garter statute of 1522 had made provision for the use of a deputy when Black Rod could not attend Garter ceremonies; but this would have been on an *ad hoc* basis. On one occasion when James Maxwell was absent in France the chief Gentleman Usher (who might ordinarily have expected to have been granted the office of Black Rod) acted in his stead at a Garter Feast at Windsor. In 1661 the Lords Journals mention for the first time a 'Yeoman Usher'; an order was made that he should not come into the chamber when the House was sitting except to inform the Gentleman Usher when a message was sent from the Commons. Two days later the Journals record a petition of John Wynyarde: 'That he having faithfully executed the Place of Yeoman Usher all the last Parliament; and, by a Warrant from the Lord High [Great] Chamberlain, being in Waiting this Parliament till Yesterday, when it was denied him to attend without the Door, by Sir John Ayton, according to their Lordships Order; he prays their Lordships will please to order him to attend without the Door, and that his exclusion from waiting within may not be a Prejudice to any Privileges or Advantages belonging to him'.

It is noteworthy that Wynyarde claimed to act by the authority of the Lord Great Chamberlain; Thayne had been appointed by Black Rod himself. Wynyarde was succeeded by Benjamin Cooling, who was appointed by Black Rod, but on his death in 1700 the question of who should appoint the Yeoman Usher became the subject of dispute: Black Rod claimed the right to make the appointment, but Cooling's son claimed that the right to the office was his by virtue of a grant from Charles II. A trial was needed to resolve the issue, and Black Rod won. To this day the formal appointment of the Yeoman Usher as his assistant is vested in Black Rod. In 1805 the Yeoman Usher was admitted as Deputy to Black Rod in his capacity as Usher of the Order of the Garter; but nowadays the Yeoman Usher has no connection with the Order of the Garter and another of the Officers of the Order would deputize in Black Rod's absence.

Notable Black Rods of the late seventeenth century included Sir Fleetwood Sheppard, Black Rod from 1695 to 1698, Nell Gwynn's steward and patron of poets. When in 1696 the Commons presented an address to the King, Sheppard, as Black Rod, invited all the members to the King's cellar where they drank the Royal health. Sheppard was succeeded by Admiral Sir David Mitchell (Black Rod 1698–1710) who had been promoted from the ranks, and who combined the office with an active career as a member of the Board of Admiralty. This was not, however, because the advent of the Yeoman Usher had made the Office of Black Rod into a sinecure—on more than one occasion Admiral Mitchell was specifically granted leave of absence by the House of Lords. Clearly he was expected normally to attend the House. Mitchell appears to be the first Black Rod to have been a high ranking member of the armed forces; later, as will be seen, it became customary to appoint a distinguished serviceman to the office.

In the later seventeenth century Black Rod received a salary of £200 a year from the Crown. He also received fees from delinquents imprisoned by him on behalf of the House of Lords, fees from Peers and probably fees on House business as well. Certainly his fees in the last category were well established by 1725—although the relationship of such fees to the actual duties performed seems to have been of very varying relevance. In 1725 Black Rod received fees from Lords taking their seats in the House according to a scale ranging from £2.10s for Barons and Bishops to £10 for Dukes (the Yeoman Usher received such fees on a smaller scale, ranging from 10s to £1.10s), and also a fee of £5 on Private Bills (the Yeoman Usher receiving £1). At this time the fee payable upon the discharge of a delinquent was £3.6s 8d.

The sequence of Black Rods in the eighteenth century was short: only six served between 1710 and 1812. Perhaps the most notable of a not very distinguished group was Sir Septimus Robinson (Black Rod 1761–1765) who had been governor of the Dukes of Gloucester and Cumberland, and had fought under Wade and Ligonier. He was succeeded by Sir Francis Molyneux, whose outstanding fame was to have held the office for almost 47 years (1765–1812), the longest tenure of any Black Rod.

Black Rod in the nineteenth century

By the beginning of the nineteenth century, the office of Black Rod had become extremely profitable. Although his fee for attending the Lords was only 6s 8d per day, and his official salary (from several sources) amounted to only a little over £300 a year, in the early years of the century his fees on the extremely numerous Private Bills often exceeded £3,000 a year. Moreover, many of Black Rod's staff of doorkeepers, housemaids, etc., were remunerated by fees which were yielding amounts quite out of proportion to the work required. Consequently, the sale of offices within his department (the duties of which might subsequently be carried out by deputies) was a profitable side line for Black Rod. In 1810 (an exceptionally good year) Black Rod (Sir Francis Molyneux) received £3,060 from the sale of offices. Molyneux's successor, Sir Thomas Tyrwhitt (Black Rod 1812–1832) was, however, persuaded to put an end to the practice of selling offices for large sums. Perhaps in some sense as a recompense, Black Rod was granted, following the recommendation of a Committee in 1827, an official residence adjoining the House of Lords. Tyrwhitt was created a Gentleman Usher only on the day before he was appointed Black Rod—obviously with a view to making the appointment. This has been the practice ever since.

An important period in the history of the office of Black Rod opened with the appointment of Sir Augustus Clifford, Black Rod from 1832 to 1877. Clifford was a Captain in the Navy at the time of his appointment (eventually being promoted to Admiral) and all subsequent appointments have been of servicemen.

To begin with, Clifford ruled over a varied group of staff. In 1850, for instance, he controlled a staff of thirty-eight, including an engineer, watchmen, housemaids, and even a 'deputy necessary woman'. As has been mentioned, many of the staff received fees in addition to their salaries, so that in 1846 the Principal Doorkeepers each received in all over £1,600, and the 'necessary woman' (all of whose duties were performed by the deputy, who received £20 a year) received nearly £800. On average the Principal Doorkeepers received about £800 a year. Not surprisingly, a Select Committee which reported in 1850 recommended that the staff be reduced and that Principal Doorkeepers appointed in future should receive a salary of £250 a year and no fees and that the offices of 'necessary woman' and 'firelighter' (another sinecure) be abolished. This reduction in the staff of Black Rod's department, however, did not affect the profitability of his office— Clifford's fees in 1866 totalled £8,875, and averaged over £5,300 between 1861 and 1875, never falling below £3,300.

Towards the end of Clifford's tenure of office there began to be irregularities in the management of the House of Lords by his staff, and reforms were made which had the effect of increasing the authority of the Lord Great Chamberlain at the expense of Black Rod. In 1876 the housekeepers, housemaids and coal porters were transferred to the control of the Lord Great Chamberlain. On Clifford's death in 1877 Black Rod's fees were abolished and replaced by a salary of £2,000 a year. In 1888 the Lord Great Chamberlain was given full charge of the 'service and custody of the House'. In 1890 the House resolved that, on a vacancy occurring in the office of Black Rod, the power of appointment of doorkeepers and messengers should also be transferred to the Lord Great Chamberlain. In 1895 Black Rod's house was appropriated for other purposes and his salary was reduced by half to £1,000.

Black Rod's decline at the end of the nineteenth century was reversed in one respect in 1906. A Select Committee reported that the House had no power to take away the appointment of doorkeepers and messengers from Black Rod, since he had this power by virtue of his patent of appointment granted by the Crown; and the House then rescinded its resolution of 1890.

During the early part of the twentieth century Black Rod's duties, apart from ceremonial ones, were confined to controlling admission of visitors to the House of Lords, and to responsibility for the Chamber, especially for the maintenance of order, during sittings. The duty of attaching delinquents had by this time ceased to be of practical importance. Despite the reduction in the powers of Black Rod, the post was held by men more distinguished than many of their predecessors—Clifford had been appointed while a Captain in the Navy, but his successor, Sir William Knollys, was a General, and his successor, Sir James Drummond, an Admiral. It then became the practice to appoint Admirals and Generals alternately, until in 1941 Air Chief Marshal Sir William Mitchell was appointed. Since then Black Rod has been appointed from the three services in rotation. Perhaps the best known of recent holders was Sir Brian Horrocks, who was previously General Officer Commanding in charge of the British Army of the Rhine, and while he was Black Rod (1949-63) became also a much loved broadcaster and orator.

During the first half of the present century the work of the Yeoman Usher increased in importance, since his post was combined with that of Secretary to the Lord Great Chamberlain, the Officer of State whose work had been so substantially increased. The Lord Great Chamberlain being an unpaid hereditary Officer of State (the office rotating among three titled families), most of his day-to-day functions were delegated to his secretary (acting under his instructions) whose responsibility for the administration of the Palace of Westminster was therefore considerable. In 1946 the two posts of Secretary and Yeoman Usher, which had been held jointly since 1896, were separated, but on the retirement two years later of the Secretary to the Lord Great Chamberlain the appointment was given again to the Yeoman Usher. In 1962 the then Yeoman Usher (Captain K. L. Mackintosh) was given a third office, that of Serjeant-at-Arms. This officer had (and has) the duty of carrying the mace before the Lord Chancellor.

This triad of offices, with a single officer being Secretary to the Lord Great Chamberlain, Yeoman Usher of the Black Rod and Serjeant-at-Arms, lasted until 1971, but the year 1965 saw important changes which substantially affected the administration of the House of Lords. Formerly the entire Palace of Westminster, as a Royal Palace, had been under the immediate control of the Crown, on whose behalf the Lord Great Chamberlain acted. In 1965, however, The Queen made over to each House of Parliament that part of the Palace of Westminster which it occupied. The control of the Royal Gallery and Robing rooms, however, remained with the Lord Great Chamberlain as representative of Her Majesty. Responsibility for the House of Lords part of the building was given to the Lord Chancellor, who vested his responsibility in the Offices Committee of the House. Initially the Administration Sub-Committee of the Offices Committee appointed Captain Mackintosh, who then held the three offices, as its agent in order to carry out the control of accommodation and services in the House of Lords part of the Palace of Westminster.

In September 1970 Air Chief Marshal Sir George Mills (Black Rod from 1963) was succeeded by Admiral Sir Frank Twiss, who had commanded the Far East fleet and served as Second Sea Lord, and in 1971 Sir Kenneth Mackintosh (as he became) retired. From January 1971 a new and simplified administration system was introduced. The Administration Sub-Committee appointed Black Rod as its agent, the Lord Great Chamberlain agreed to his appointment as his secretary, and the post of Serjeant-at-Arms was amalgamated with that of Black Rod. Sir Frank Twiss combined the offices of Black Rod, Serjeant-at-Arms, Secretary to the Lord Great Chamberlain and agent of the Administration Sub-Committee. This arrangement continued when Sir Frank Twiss was succeeded as Black Rod in 1978 by Lieutenant-General Sir David House, previously General Officer Commanding, Northern Ireland. The nature of Black Rod's duties under this new administrative system will be described in the next section.

Duties of Black Rod today

1   Black Rod's primary duty remains that originally specified in the Statute of the Order of the Garter of 1522, 'the Care and Custody, and Pre-eminence of keeping' of the doors of the High Court of Parliament. By virtue of this provision Black Rod has power to admit persons to the House of Lords and to exclude them if the House (or the Sovereign when present) so orders. In exercise of this authority Black Rod appoints and controls the Doorkeepers of the House, of whom there are twenty-three, and regulates the galleries and the issuing of admission tickets to visitors.

2   Black Rod also has a disciplinary function— he is responsible for maintaining order within the precincts of the House and, if necessary, for taking into custody 'any person whom the House may order to be detained'. The House has not in fact made such an order since 1870, but formerly did so frequently. Thus in 1806 one William Broadhurst was detained by Black Rod, and brought before the House, for insulting one of the doorkeepers 'in the execution of his duty in Westminster Hall'. If the House resolved to keep an offender in custody, Black Rod would again be responsible for detaining him if the detention was to be for a short period only, but if the detention were to be for more than a short time Black Rod would convey the prisoner to the appropriate civil authority.

3   Black Rod attends the House when it is sitting, and, subject to the directions of the House, is responsible for the maintenance of order within the Chamber. Black Rod sits in a box immediately below the bar on the right hand side of the Chamber (as one faces the throne). Either he or the Yeoman Usher has to be present during sittings of the House. When a division is called he switches on (in his box) the division bells which sound in the precincts of the House to warn Lords who are not in the Chamber.

4   As agent of the Administration Sub-Committee, Black Rod is responsible for the allocation and maintenance of accommodation and services and the control of security in that part of the Palace of Westminster used by the House.

5   As Secretary to the Lord Great Chamberlain, Black Rod is responsible for the Royal Apartments of the Palace of Westminster—that is to say, for the Queen's Robing Room (used at State Openings of Parliament), for the Royal Gallery (through which The Queen walks in procession on her way from the Robing Room to the House of Lords) and, in conjunction with the Lord Chancellor and Mr Speaker, for Westminster Hall. As Secretary to the Lord Great Chamberlain, Black Rod is responsible for the administration of the Crypt Chapel and keeps the Chapel registers. He is also responsible for administrative arrangements when the Sovereign is in Parliament.

6   Finally, in addition to these varied and important administrative duties at Westminster, Black Rod has ceremonial duties which make him a well-known figure to the public at large.

i   He participates in the annual Garter ceremonies at Windsor (see page 2).

ii   In the House of Lords, his first ceremonial activity is his own introduction. After prayers are over at the beginning of a sitting, the Leader of the House of Lords (a member of the Government) announces the appointment officially to the House. The old Black Rod leaves his box immediately below the Bar of the House, bows and withdraws. The new Black Rod, wearing his chain of office and carrying the Black Rod, advances (having been waiting in the lobby), bows and takes his place in the box.

iii   As Serjeant-at-Arms it is his duty to carry the Mace before the Lord Chancellor when he enters the House in procession at the beginning of each sitting. In practice the Yeoman Usher, who is deputy Serjeant-at-Arms, normally fulfils this function. Black Rod himself follows the Lord Chancellor's procession into the Chamber and takes up his position in his box.

iv   When a new Peer is introduced into the House of Lords, Black Rod leads the procession (which includes the Peer and his two supporters and a herald) into and out of the House.

PLATE 2 : *Black Rod, Sir George Mills (fifth from the front in the right hand file),
carries the Rod in the Queen's procession at the State Opening of Parliament.*

v Black Rod's best known ceremonial function is the summoning of the
House of Commons on behalf of the Sovereign. The most important
occasion on which he does this is at the State Opening of Parliament, when
the Commons are called to hear the Queen's Speech. There are however
other occasions when the Commons attend in the House of Lords. At the
beginning of each new Parliament, before the State Opening, they are
called to hear the Lord Chancellor, on behalf of the Queen, order them to
choose a Speaker, and next day they return to have their choice approved,
again by the Lord Chancellor in the Queen's name. At the end of each

11

session of Parliament there is a further 'Queen's Speech', but made on her behalf by the Lord Chancellor. Finally, the Royal Assent to Bills may be given by Royal Commission, in which case the Commons are summoned by Black Rod to hear the Commission read. (Since 1967, however, it has been more usual for the Royal Assent to be notified by a simple announcement to each House separately by the Lord Chancellor and the Speaker.)

When Black Rod goes to summon the Commons an elaborate ritual is followed. Black Rod, if The Queen is present, is told to summon the Commons by the Lord Great Chamberlain, who raises his white wand of office. When The Queen is not present the Lord Chancellor, speaking for the Lords Commissioners, orally commands him to let the Commons know that their immediate attendance is required. Black Rod then walks down the Peers' corridor, through the Central Lobby and down the Commons corridor to the Members' Lobby, preceded by the Superintendent of Custodians and a Lords Doorkeeper. The police keep a gangway clear for him through the Central Lobby, and the Assistant Serjeant at Arms in the Commons, Commons Doorkeepers and police form a gangway through the Members' Lobby. As Black Rod enters the Members' Lobby Doorkeepers close the western half of the door of the Commons Chamber (open until then) and turn the bolt of the eastern half

PLATE 4 : *Black Rod, Sir George Mills, summons the members of the House of Commons to hear The Queen's speech.*

ready for the Serjeant at Arms of the House of Commons to slam it. As Black Rod crosses the Lobby the door is slammed in his face. He then knocks three times on the door, after which the Serjeant at Arms looks through a grille in the door, which is then opened (*see plate 3*). Black Rod is announced, he enters, bows at the bar, advances to the Table of the House, and summons the Commons, who return with him (*see plates 4, 5*). (It is said that on one occasion Sir Augustus Clifford lost his hat and suffered an injury to his arm owing to the pressure of Members of Parliament rushing to get places in the House of Lords.)

The ritual of summons is supposed to be an assertion by the Commons of their independence of the Sovereign (and, therefore, of her representative). When it originated is not clear. It certainly ante-dates the attempted arrest of the five Members in 1642, though the Commons appear to have attached particular importance to it during the latter part of the reign of Charles I—the Commons Journals of the 1640s often record the ritual in more detail than they have since. And on 10th May 1641, as has been seen, when Black Rod, arriving with a message without his Black Rod, came in before he was called, exception was taken at both. The insistence that Black Rod should not enter until admitted is, however, no more than a gesture, for a Speaker's ruling in 1962 confirmed that the House has no power to refuse admission to Black Rod when he has knocked three times—all other business of whatever kind in the Commons must immediately cease.

PLATE 5 : *Black Rod, Sir Frank Twiss, with Mr Speaker, leads the Commons to the House of Lords to hear The Queen's speech.*

Antiquities of the Office of Black Rod

1 *The Rod*

The earliest known mention of the Rod is in the patent of 1361 granting 12d a day to Walter Whitehorse, which refers to his duty to bear the Rod before the King in processions on Feast days. The statute of 1522 relating to Black Rod describes the Rod as having at one end 'the Lion the Ensign of the English', a feature retained on the present Rod. Although the custom this century has been for the Rod to be handed on to successive Black Rods, in the past it seems to have been retained by former Black Rods or their families. A rod made for Sir Thomas Duppa (Black Rod 1683–1694) is still in the possession of his family. There is record of a Rod having been made in 1710 for Sir William Oldes (newly appointed Black Rod) and of another having been made for his successor, Sir William Saunderson, in 1718. It is recorded that in 1832 two Rods were ordered for Sir Augustus Clifford on his appointment as Black Rod.

The present Rod dates from 1883 (as the hallmark indicates), although details have been altered since. It is three and a half feet long, and of ebony. At one end (the top) is a gold lion holding a shield, surmounted by a Crown, and bearing the initials E vii R. It is surrounded by the garter bearing the motto 'Honi soit qui mal y pense'. At the centre of the Rod is a gold orb embossed with oak leaves. At the bottom end is a gold knob surmounted by a 1904 gold sovereign; the side visible is the reverse, which shows Saint George on horseback, slaying the dragon (*see plates 6, 7 and 8*). The design of the Rod seems to have altered little since the seventeenth century; the Rod made for Sir Thomas Duppa, though it is slightly less ornate than the present Rod, is essentially similar.

2 *Chain of Office*

For both Garter and Parliamentary ceremonies Black Rod wears his gold chain of office. On the chain hangs a badge of office, which consists of a gold knot surrounded by the garter (with motto) and surmounted by a Crown. The wearing of the badge and chain was first ordained by Queen Elizabeth I in 1566 (though a different form of badge had been worn by Sir Philip Hoby, Black Rod 1543-1554). The present badge and chain are not hallmarked, but seem to date from the late nineteenth century *(see plate 9)*.

3   Robes

When attending the House of Lords Black Rod wears court dress—black shoes with black buckles, silk stockings, black breeches, and black coat with a black 'wig bag' at the back. In addition he wears a sword in a black scabbard. The Chain is worn and the Rod carried only on ceremonial occasions. At State Openings of Parliament ruffles are worn at the wrists and a jabot at the neck.

When taking part in Garter ceremonies Black Rod wears the scarlet mantle of an Officer of the Order of the Garter, adorned on the left shoulder with a Garter badge, and a black velvet cap. Over his robes he wears his chain of office. He carries the Black Rod.

PLATES 6, 7 AND 8 : *Parts of the Black Rod: the gold lion at the top; the orb at the centre; and the gold knob (with 1904 sovereign) at the bottom.*
PLATE 9 : *The chain and badge of office of Black Rod.*

Holders of the Office of Gentleman Usher of the Black Rod 1361—1981

(Unless otherwise indicated the date given is the date of the letters patent of appointment)

By 1361	Whitehorse, Walter
8 May 1387	Cray, John
9 Dec 1399	Sy, Thomas
26 Nov 1410	Sheffield, John
18 Sep 1413	Athelbrigg, John
16 Oct 1415	Hargrove, William
17 Sep 1418	Clifford, John
3 Mar 1423	Carsons, John
8 Mar 1428	Pope, William
26 Jul 1438	{ Pope, William Manfeld, Robert
28 Apr 1459[1]	Penycok, John
1 Apr 1461	Maulevrer, Halnath
20 Jul 1471	Evington, William
24 May 1483	{ Evington, William Hardgill, Edward
20 Sep 1485	Marleton, Robert
1 Feb 1489	Assheton, Ralph
19 Nov 1495	{ Assheton, Ralph Dennys, Hugh
4 Feb 1513	Compton, William *knighted 1513*
23 Oct 1526	Norris, Henry
9 Dec 1536	Knyvett, Anthony
3 Nov 1543	Hoby, Philip *knighted 1544*
1 May 1554	{ Norris, John *died 1565* Norris, William
28 May 1591	Wingfield, Anthony
14 Jul 1593	Bowyer, Simon
24 Apr 1598	Coningsby, Richard *knighted 1603*
17 Oct 1605	{ Coningsby, Richard, kt. Pollard, George
1620[2]	Maxwell, James

12 Sep 1642[3]	{Maxwell, James {Thayne, Alexander
2 Mar 1645[4]	Newton, Peter
14 Jan 1661[5]	Ayton, John *later knighted*
Jan 1671[6]	Carteret, Edward, kt.
Mar 1683[6]	Duppa, Thomas *knighted 1683*
25 Apr 1694	Sheppard, Fleetwood, kt.
5 Dec 1698	Mitchell, David, kt.
10 Jul 1710	Oldes, William, kt.
10 Nov 1718	Saunderson, William, kt. *created baronet, 1720*
26 May 1727	Dalton, Charles, kt.
1 Oct 1747	Bellenden, Hon. Henry *knighted 1749*
16 Apr 1761	Robinson, Septimus, kt.
18 Sep 1765	Molyneux, Francis, kt. *succeeded as 7th baronet, 1781*
11 Jun 1812	Tyrwhitt, Thomas, kt.
25 Jul 1832	Clifford, Augustus William James, kt. *created baronet, 1838*
31 Mar 1877	Knollys, William Thomas, kt.
Jul 1883[6]	Drummond, Hon. James Robert, kt.
16 Dec 1895	Biddulph, Michael Anthony Shrapnel, kt.
24 Jul 1904	Stephenson, Henry Frederick, kt.
1 Jan 1920	Pulteney, William, kt.
26 Sep 1941	Mitchell, William Gore Sutherland, kt.
1 Jan 1945	Blake, Geoffrey, kt.
18 Jan 1949	Horrocks, Brian Gwynne, kt.
18 Jun 1963	Mills, George Holroyd, kt.
1 Sep 1970	Twiss, Frank Roddam, kt.
16 Jan 1978	House, David George, kt.

1 On 17 July 1459 John Penycok the younger was granted the reversion of the office. There is no evidence that he ever succeeded to it.

2 Succeeded by virtue of a grant in reversion 24 Apr 1617.

3 After 1642 Maxwell and Thayne remained in the service of the House of Lords at Westminster.

4 Date of admission. Newton was in the service of the King.

5 Date of admission.

6 Date of letters patent not traced.

Other Rods

1 *Black Rods in other legislative assemblies*

The earliest occurrence of a 'Black Rod' outside the House of Lords was in the Irish House of Lords. He is mentioned in the first printed Journal of the House in 1634 and that he was intended to be modelled precisely on the English Black Rod is suggested by a dispute in 1646 as to the right of appointment of an Irish Yeoman Usher, information being obtained from England in order to settle the matter. The Parliamentary duties of the Irish Black Rods ceased with the abolition of the Irish Parliament in 1800. The newly created Senate of Northern Ireland had a Black Rod, however, from its institution in 1921 until direct rule was introduced.

As legislative assemblies with Upper Houses were established in Commonwealth countries during the nineteenth century certain of them appointed Black Rods as their disciplinary officers, amongst them New South Wales, Queensland, Tasmania, Victoria, Western Australia, New Zealand, Cape of Good Hope, Natal, Quebec, Newfoundland, Prince Edward Island, Canada, Jamaica, Tobago, the Commonwealth of Australia (in 1901) and South Africa (in 1910). South Australia appointed its first Black Rod in 1953.

2 *White Rod*

As early as 1393 a grant was made to Sir Alexander Cockburn and his heirs of the office of Principal Usher of the King of Scotland at Parliaments, General Councils, and feasts. The Usher continued to attend the Parliament until it ceased to exist on the Union of England and Scotland in 1707, but his duties appear to have been primarily ceremonial. He was responsible for seeing that strangers were cleared and the doors closed before Parliament sat. He carried a white rod before the King in procession, and he became known as the Usher of the White Rod.

After 1707 White Rod continued to be entitled to a salary and to fees from newly created peers, baronets and knights, and he sometimes participated in Coronation processions. Until the latter part of the eighteenth century the office remained in the hands of the Cockburn family (though there was a dispute over the entitlement to the office in the early part of the seventeenth century) but it was then sold. After passing through several hands the office was eventually purchased in 1806 by Sir Patrick Walker. After his death in 1837 the office was held first by his two sisters jointly, then by the survivor of them and then by their trustees, who continued to receive the salary of the office until 1897. In that year the Treasury commuted the salary, but not the fees, which continued to be received.

3 Rods in other orders of Knighthood

Black Rod is the most ancient and famous office of a rod-bearer in Britain but Ushers have been appointed who bear rods in other orders of Knighthood.

ORDER OF THE THISTLE

The Order of the Thistle was revived in 1687 and in 1714 the Knights Brethren complained that there was as yet no Usher appointed in conformity with the Statutes of the Order. Accordingly, on their recommendation, Thomas Brand was appointed Usher of the Green Rod, knighted, and made an extra Gentleman Usher to the King. George I also acceded to a request of the Knights 'that as the Usher of the Black Rod is, in honour of the Order of the Garter, the first Gentleman Usher daily Waiter, so the Usher of the Thistle, or Green Rod, might also be second Gentleman Usher daily Waiter, in honour of the Thistle'. George II duly reappointed Brand, but George III did not, and subsequent Gentlemen Ushers of the Green Rod were not, in fact, Gentleman Ushers. It is interesting to note that two subsequent appointees, Robert Quarme and his son (also Robert) were in addition Yeomen Ushers of the Black Rod.

ORDER OF THE BATH

Upon its revival in 1725 an Usher was appointed for the Order of the Bath, and given the title Gentleman Usher of the Scarlet (or Red) Rod.

ORDER OF ST. PATRICK

The Order of St. Patrick was instituted in 1783, and provided with an Usher of the Black Rod from its institution. Sir N. H. Nicolas (*Orders of Knighthood of the British Empire*) provides a list of Ushers up to the 1840s, and up to 1800 two of the four appointees named appear also to have been Black Rod in the Irish House of Lords. After the demise of the Irish House of Lords in 1800, appointments continued to be made to the office of Usher of the Black Rod of the Order of St. Patrick until 1918. When that appointee died in 1933 he was not replaced.

ORDER OF ST. MICHAEL AND ST. GEORGE

The Order of St. Michael and St. George was founded in 1818, but only acquired a 'Rod' in 1911, when the King granted to the Officer of Arms of the Order the title of 'Gentleman Usher of the Blue Rod'.

ORDER OF THE BRITISH EMPIRE

The Order of the British Empire was instituted in 1917, and the Officers appointed in 1918 included a 'Gentleman Usher of the Purple Rod'.

Select Bibliography

The main source for the history of Black Rod is the series of *Journals of the House of Lords,* 1510 to date, supplemented by the classes of Parliament Office Papers, Committee records, and Black Rod's records which are preserved in the House of Lords Record Office. The following works have also been consulted in the preparation of this booklet:

Anstis, John, *The Register of the Order of the Garter* (1724).

Ashmole, Elias, *The Institution, Laws and Ceremonies of the Most Noble Order of the Garter* (1672).

Horrocks, Sir Brian, 'Gentleman Usher of the Black Rod' in *Journal of the Society of Clerks-at-the-Table in Empire Parliaments,* vol. xix (1950), pp. 128-131.

Nicolas, Sir Nicholas Harris, *History of the Orders of Knighthood of the British Empire . . .* (1841)

Royle, Sir Guy, 'Holders of the Office of Gentleman Usher of the Black Rod 1361-1948' in *Notes and Queries,* vol cxciii (1948), pp.96-97.

Sainty, J. C., *Officers of the House of Lords 1485 to 1971,* House of Lords Record Office Memorandum No. 45 (1971).

Saxon, A. W., 'New South Wales: Presentation of a Black Rod to the Legislative Council and Visit of the Prince of Wales' in *The Table,* vol. xliii (1975), pp. 52-54.

Thorne, Peter, *Ceremonial and the Mace in the House of Commons,* House of Commons Library Document No. 11 (1980).

[anon.], *Black Rod* (New South Wales, 1974).

Printed in England by Robendene Ltd, Amersham
and published by Her Majesty's Stationery Office
Dd 716579 C30 7/81